CLASSICAL MUSIC FOR THE

CHURCH SERVICE

VOLUME 1
EARLY INTERMEDIATE

Piano Literature Appropriate for the Worship Service

EDITED BY MAURICE HINSON

Alfred

Contents

Foreword

Although the organ has historically been the principal instrument of church worship, its role has been taken over by the piano in many churches. Many churches use the piano as their main musical instrument, and many have a piano located in the sanctuary or in smaller chapels and educational rooms.

Classical music, specifically music from the 17th through the 19th centuries, is frequently used in churches and is appropriate for many types of worship services. Keyboard music from the Baroque period, for example, is easily assimilated in the worship service because of its linear elements and serious character. Composers such as J. S. Bach, Mendelssohn and Franck wrote a great deal of music for the church, and much of their keyboard music fits easily into a church service. Their music contains lasting value and has withstood the test of time.

The purpose of this three-volume series is to provide the pianist classical music appropriate to the worship service. Many pianists study classical music and their talents can and should be used in church services. The editor grew up attending a church that encouraged him to use his classical piano training by playing preludes, offertories, solos and postludes in religious services. These collections present music that falls within the technical capacity of the intermediate pianist. For this music to be effective, the pianist must feel comfortable with it both technically and interpretatively. A piece that is sufficiently prepared is a piece that will probably be performed well in the church service. Therefore, information is given about each piece to help the pianist approach it as musically as possible.

Criteria for Selecting Piano Music for Church Use

1. Melody
Melody is very obvious to most ears, and flowing melody helps create an appropriate atmosphere in a service. Thus, diatonic melodies are desirable, and those that are disjunct, highly fluid or very chromatic should be avoided.

2. Harmony
A great deal of harmonic variety can be found in good church music. However, there are limits, harmonically speaking, to what is generally considered acceptable for most services. Music that incorporates a great deal of dissonance should be avoided, as should pieces that use harmonies and progressions associated with blues, jazz and rock. Aleatoric and 12-tone works also are generally not acceptable as church music.

3. Rhythm and Tempo
Highly syncopated music is not appropriate for worship services. Too many unusual rhythmic stresses hinder a smooth musical flow. Music that ranges from slow to moderately fast will probably be better suited to most services than very fast music.

4. Dynamics
Good church piano music will have a balance between piano and forte. Short excursions into pianissimo and fortissimo can also be desirable. A piece that uses fortissimo for long periods may tend to demostrate virtuosity and have a showy character. Virtuosity places too much emphasis on the performer and detracts from the worship atmosphere.

5. Form
Good formal structure is essential. Intelligible shape is necessary to any art.

6. Articulation and Touch
Legato and cantabile pieces are generally more suitable to the worship service than pieces that use a great deal of staccato and drastic articulation changes.

7. Title
The title usually gives the composer's idea(s) of the mood and/or character of the piece. Religious titles such as "Prayer," "Reconciliation" and "Andante Religioso" indicate music that is probably suitable for church use. Works with titles similar to these are probably suitable.

8. Association
It is best to avoid pieces which have strong secular connotations, as do most popularized classics. For example, Debussy's *"Clair de lune"* is a beautiful piece, but has strong secular associations which may be distracting—perhaps the listeners have heard it at a piano recital, or it may recall a movie that used this piece, etc. Works associated with opera, movies or television should not be used.

9. Appropriateness
Always consider the type of service (morning worship, communion, youth group), as well as the cultural, ethnic and social background of the congregation, when selecting music.

About this Edition

These collections contain music that meets the above criteria for selecting piano music for church use. They are practical performer's editions and provide repertoire for amateur or professional musicians, and for students in elementary through high school. This repertoire can be used in recitals and for leisure playing, as well as in religious services.

In compiling these collections, the editor has used the most reliable sources available. All editorial indications are included in parentheses. Fingering is editorial, as are pedal indications, with exceptions listed in footnotes. All metronome marks are editorial as well, and are only suggestions. Ornaments are realized in the score or in footnotes. The editor's marks may need to be modified to suit the acoustics of a particular room or church sanctuary. The pianist should pay careful attention and try to avoid a thick, muddy sound. The una corda (soft) pedal may be especially effective in pianissimo (***pp***) passages. Much of the music in this collection is excellent for developing a cantabile (singing) tone on the piano.

Original titles have been used with each piece. A suggested second title, enclosed in Parenthesis, is included with some of the pieces. This second title may be more appropriate for a specific church service and may be used in church bulletins. If an opus number or other identification is listed in this collection, it should be used in the bulletin as well.

Pieces are arranged alphabetically by composer. A suggested classification for use (preludes, offertories, solos, postludes) of the pieces in this collection is listed on page 10. Many of the pieces may be used for more than one function, i.e., the same piece may serve well for a prelude and offertory, etc.

This volume is dedicated to Dr. and Mrs. Wesley Roberts,
with appreciation and admiration.

Maurice Hinson

About the Pieces

ANONYMOUS

Entrance *Page 12*

This cheerful piece is found in the *Notebook for Wolfgang* by Leopold Mozart (1762). Take both repeats and vary dynamics on the repeat.

GOTTFRIED HEINRICH BACH (1724–1761)

Air in F, BWV Anh. 131 *Page 13*

This Bach was the eldest son of Johann Sebastian and Anna Magdalena Bach. Keep this piece flowing easily throughout and observe the repeats. Clear articulation is absolutely necessary.

JOHANN SEBASTIAN BACH (1685–1750)

Aria, BWV 515 *Page 14*

This flowing aria from the Notebook for Anna Magdalena must never sound rushed. Vary the dynamics on each repeat.

Choral, BWV 514 *Page 15*

Bach left only the outer voices for this choral in the *Notebook for Anna Magdalena.* The editor has filled in the harmony. Quick pedal changes will keep the harmonies clear.

JOHANN FRIEDRICH BURGMÜLLER (1806–1874)

Pastorale, Op. 100, No. 3 *Page 16*

Keep the repeated left-hand chords quieter than the right-hand melody. Bring out the left hand at measure 15.

Tender Flower, Op. 100, No. 10 *Page 18*

Effective articulation of two-note slurs is essential for a successful performance of this piece. Lift the hand slightly and quickly after the second note has been played. Notice the small dynamic range used throughout.

JOHANN HEINRICH BUTTSTEDT (1666–1727)

Arietta *Page 20*

This little two-voice song contains much charm. The editor suggests: (1) play as written, (2) repeat, playing one octave higher, and (3) play as written.

FRÉDÉRIC CHOPIN (1810–1849)

Prelude in C Minor, Op. 28, No. 20 *Page 21*

This famous piece requires good arm weight throughout, especially in measures 5–13, to ensure that each note sounds. The top note of each chord should sound slightly louder than the rest of the chord. Pedal each chord change.

VICTOR ALPHONSE DUVERNOY (1842–1907)

Melody, Op. 176, No. 3 *Page 22*

The right-hand melodic line should flow and sing throughout. Voice the right hand slightly louder than the left hand.

CÉSAR FRANCK (1822–1890)

Old Christmas Carol *Page 24*

This expressive carol requires careful pedaling, especially because of the eighth notes. Make your listeners aware of the two-measure phrasing that begins at measure 16.

Prayer *Page 25*

Frequent pedal changes are necessary in this piece. Make the "hairpin" dynamics obvious, but expressive.

Song from the Creuse *Page 26*

The Creuse is an area in central France and the name of a river that flows through that area. Notice the asymmetrical phrase structure of this piece: 2 measures+2+1, 2+1, etc. The reharmonizations are charming. The final three measures must be the quietest in the piece.

ENRIQUE GRANADOS (1867–1916)

Dedication, Op. 1, No. 1 *Page 27*

Be careful that the syncopated melody in measures 9 and 11 remains very smooth. Take a little more time with these two measures. Careful legato pedal throughout is necessary.

EDVARD GRIEG (1843–1907)

Lullaby from Valders *Page 28*

Valders is a province of Norway. Measures 1–8 and 9–16 may be repeated. The grace notes in measures 10 and 12 should be played before the beat.

CORNELIUS GURLITT (1820–1901)

Andantino, Op. 205, No. 1 *Page 30*

This melody-oriented piece requires plenty of time at measures 14–16, with an a tempo at measure 17. Op. 205 is entitled "Little Flowers," but names of flowers are not provided for the individual numbers.

Moderato, Op. 205, No. 2 *Page 31*

Make careful distinctions between each indicated dynamic level. Repeat the entire piece.

GEORGE FRIDERIC HANDEL (1685–1759)

Sarabande *Page 32*

Vary the dynamics on repeats and observe the articulation carefully. Arpeggiate the final chord on the repeat.

GÉNARI KARGANOV (1858–1890)

Prayer *Page 33*

Organ sonorities are brought to mind by this piece. Perfect legato is required throughout. Make the pianissimo at measure 13 as effective as possible.

THEODOR FÜRCHTEGOTT KIRCHNER (1823–1903)

Album Leaf, from Op. 7 *Page 34*

Observe all repeats and keep the dynamic range quite restricted. Hold all of the chords marked "ten." (tenuto) slightly longer. Bring out the descending bass line in measures 1–7 and 25–31.

Tranquil and Expressive, Op. 62, No. 8 *Page 35*

This piece is from a set entitled *Miniatures.* Observe both repeats and bring out the inner voices the second time through. A restful quality should pervade the work.

JOHANN PHILIPP KIRNBERGER (1721–1783)

Moderato *Page 36*

This little contrapuntal piece contains very interesting, flowing lines. Vary dynamics on repeats, including a slight ritardando in the final measure.

FELIX MENDELSSOHN (1809–1847)
Andante Sostenuto, Op. 72, No. 2 *Page 37*
This piece comes from a set entitled *Six Pieces for Young People.* Emphasize the melodic line throughout and keep the contrasting accompaniment quiet. Inner voices add interest at measures 13 and 26–32.

WOLFGANG AMADEUS MOZART (1756–1791)
Allegro in B-flat Major, K. 3 *Page 40*
This two-voice piece requires special attention to articulation: carefully observe the two-note slurs.

CHRISTIAN GOTTLOB NEEFE (1748–1798)
Canzonet (Song) *Page 42*
Neefe taught the young Beethoven. Left-hand quarter notes may be played slightly detached despite the slurs. Vary dynamics on the repeat.

HENRY PURCELL (1659–1695)
Air in D Minor *Page 43*
Half and dotted-half notes add much harmonic interest to this piece, so be sure they get full value. Repeat the piece and vary the dynamics.

ALEXANDER REINAGLE (1756–1809)
Andante, Op. 2, No. 2 *Page 44*
This piece is from a set entitled *A Second Set of Short and Easy Lessons.* The left hand should generally be quieter than the right hand. Measure 31 should be played with rhythmic precision like measure 15.

CARL REINECKE (1824–1910)
Elegy, from Op. 183 *Page 45*
This piece is from a larger work entitled *Serenade No. 2.* Repeat the piece and vary dynamics. Notice the accents on beat 3 of measures 1 and 17; give slightly more emphasis at these points.

Prelude, from Op. 183 *Page 46*
This piece is from a larger work entitled *Serenade No. 1.* A lovely melody is contained in the second 16th of the right-hand groups. Take a small ritardando at measure 16; repeat the entire piece.

Song, from Op. 183 *Page 47*
This piece is also from *Serenade No. 1.* Keep measure 20 strictly in time, followed by a slight ritardando at measure 21.

DOMENICO SCARLATTI (1685–1757)
Larghetto, K. 34 *Page 48*
This short sonata requires a slow tempo to bring out its inherent majestic quality. Follow the realized ornamentation carefully.

Sonata in D Minor, K. 32 *Page 50*
Repeat both halves and vary dynamics. Be sure the 32nd and 16th figures are rhythmically accurate.

FRANZ SCHUBERT (1797–1828)

Andante Page 51

This piece was composed in 1825, and even though it is short, it contains the essence of Schubert's style: a beautiful melody, lovely harmony and effective syncopation. Repeat each section and aim for harmonic clarity with the pedal.

ROBERT SCHUMANN (1810–1856)

Chorale, Op. 68, No. 4 Page 52

This piece is from the *Album for the Young.* It requires careful pedal technique throughout, plus sensitive finger substitution.

A Famous Melody by Beethoven Page 53

This interesting piece was originally planned for the *Album for the Young,* although it never made it into the final collection. Make sure the fortissimo in measure 12 receives a strong accent.

Little Cradle Song, Op. 124, No. 6. Page 54

This piece comes from the set entitled *Album Leaves.* The right hand contains both melody and accompaniment. Be sure that the two are carefully delineated by giving the first note of each triplet its full time value and slightly more stress.

Little Study, Op. 124, No. 6 Page 56

The right hand contains both melody and broken chord figures, while the left-hand part provides appropriate harmony. Long lines and dynamic variation are essential to the interpretation of this piece.

Melody, Op. 68, No. 1 Page 58

The right hand contains a charming and flowing melody. Give more emphasis to the right hand first note in measures 5–7 and 13–15. A slight ritardando in the final measure is appropriate.

Norse Song, Op. 68, No. 40 Page 59

This piece is dedicated to the Danish composer Neils Gade (1817–1890). The melody notes of measures 1, 5, 13 and 17, plus the bass notes of measure 9, spell his name G A D E. Careful legato pedaling is necessary.

PETER ILYICH TCHAIKOVSKY (1840–1893)

In Church, Op. 39, No. 23 Page 60

Vary the repeated chords slightly. Make the right-hand melody from measure 33 to the end more prominent than the repeated left-hand E. The left-hand countermelody at measure 37 to the end should be brought out slightly, thereby producing a duet between the hands.

Morning Prayer, Op. 39, No. 1 Page 62

Both Tchaikovsky pieces are from his *Album for the Young.* This piece requires an elegant legato and careful use of the pedal.

DANIEL GOTTLOB TÜRK (1750–1813)

Serious Feelings Page 63

This piece comes from *Handstücke für angehende Klavierspieler I* (1792). Repeat both sections and use pedal to enhance the legato.

JOHANN GEORG WITTHAUER (1751–1802)

Andantino Page 64

Keep the tempo flowing, but not too fast. Repeat both sections and vary the dynamics. The pedal should only be used where indicated.

Suggested Classifications for Use of the Pieces

PRELUDES

OFFERTORIES

Entrance

Anonymous

ⓐ Dynamics are editorial.

Air in F

Gottfried Heinrich Bach
BWV Anh. 131

(♩ = c. 126)

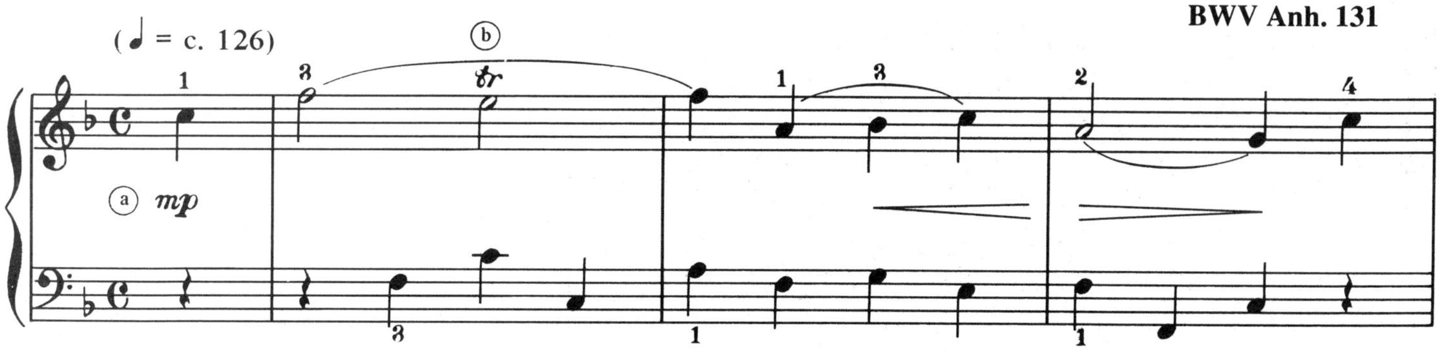

ⓐ Dynamics are editorial.

ⓑ 

Aria

Johann Sebastian Bach
BWV 515

(♩ = c. 104)

ⓐ Dynamics are editorial.

Choral

Johann Sebastian Bach
BWV 514

(Andante ♩ = c. 88)

ⓐ Dynamics are editorial.

Pastorale

Johann Friedrich Burgmüller
Op. 100, No. 3

14
ten.
17
p dolce
(pp)
20
23
cresc.
26
p
dim. e poco rall.
pp

Tender Flower

(Alternate title: Moderato)

Johann Friedrich Burgmüller
Op. 100, No. 10

Moderato (♩ = c. 108)

13
(cresc.
mf)
dim. e poco rall.
16
a tempo
p delicato
19
22
dim. e poco rall.

Arietta

Johann Heinrich Buttstedt

Andante (♩ = c. 96)

ⓐ Dynamics are editorial.

Prélude in C Minor

Frédéric Chopin
Op. 28, No. 20

Melody

Victor Alphonse Duvernoy
Op. 176, No. 3

(♩ = c. 104)

12
1
(p)
(pp)
15
5
3
(mp)
p
5
18
5
3
1
4
21
3
(cresc.)

Old Christmas Carol

César Franck

Prayer

Quasi lento (♩ = c. 88)

César Franck

Song from the Creuse

César Franck

Dedication

Enrique Granados
Op. 1, No. 1

Andantino (♩ = c. 72)

Lullaby from Valders

(Alternate title: Song from Valders)

Edvard Grieg

Moderately (♩ = c. 58)

13
cresc.
dim.
17
p
21
f
24
p
pp

Andantino

Cornelius Gurlitt
Op. 205, No. 1

Moderato

Cornelius Gurlitt
Op. 205, No. 2

(♩ = c. 104)

Sarabande

(Alternate title: Prelude)

George Friedrich Handel

Moderately (♩ = c. 100)

Prayer

Génari Karganov

Moderato e cantabile (♩ = c. 88)

Album Leaf

Theodor Kirchner
from Op. 7

Quiet, delicate (♩ = c. 88)

Tranquil and Expressive

Theodor Kirchner
Op. 62, No. 8

Ruhig, ausdrucksvoll (♪ = c. 112)

Moderato

Johann Philipp Kirnberger

Andante Sostenuto

Felix Mendelssohn
Op. 72, No. 2

(♩ = c. 66)

13
cresc.
16
f
19
dim.
p
22
p
25
cresc.

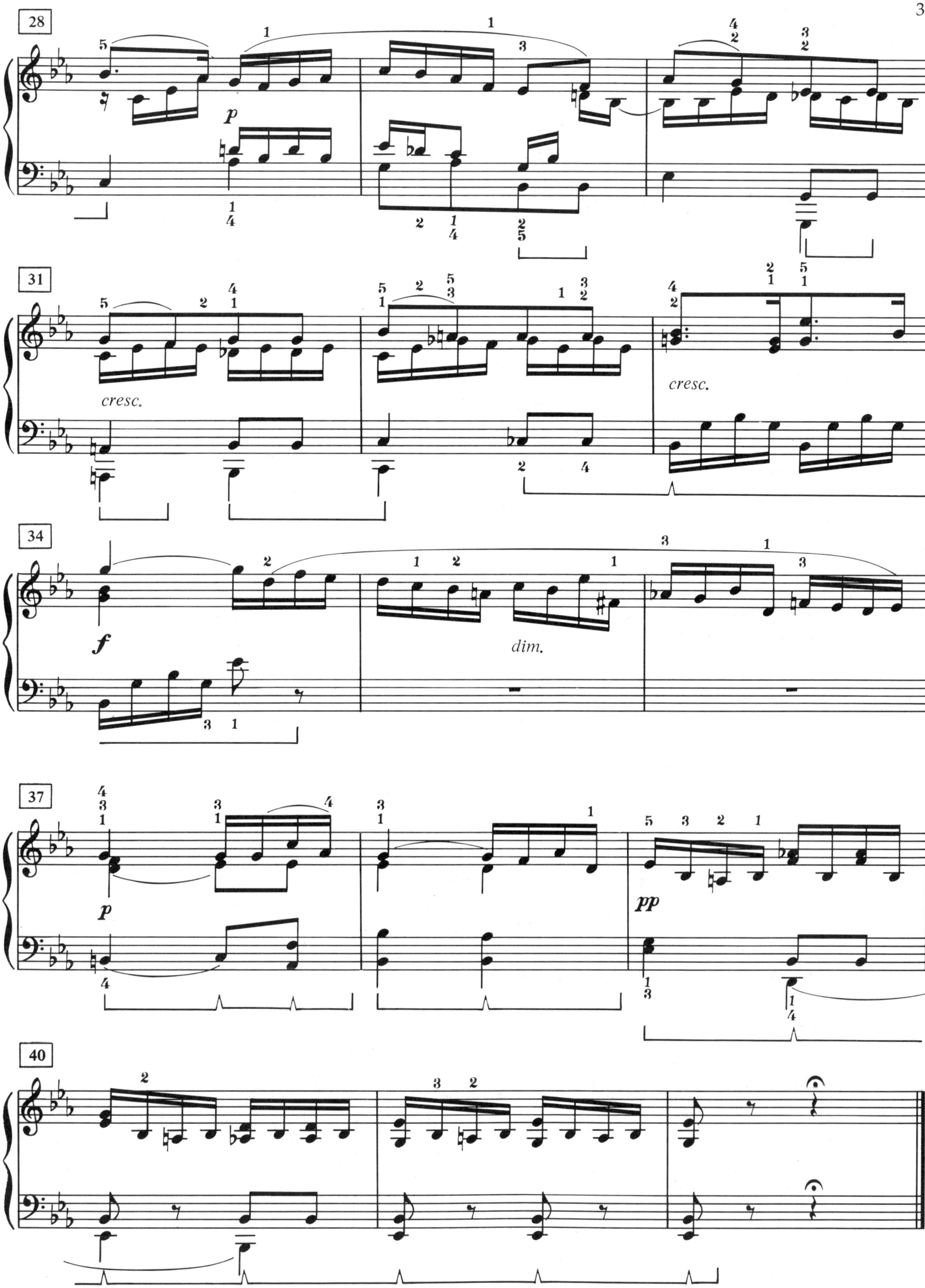
28
31
cresc.
cresc.
34
dim.
37
40

Allegro in B-flat Major

Wolfgang Amadeus Mozart
K. 3

Allegro (♩ = c. 66)

ⓐ Dynamics are editorial.

(poco rit.)

Canzonet

(Song)

Christian Gottlob Neefe

Moderato cantabile (♩ = c. 120)

ⓐ Dynamics are editorial.

Air in D Minor

Henry Purcell

Andante (♩ = c. 108)

ⓐ Phrase marks are editorial.

Andante

Alexander Reinagle
Op. 2, No. 2

(♩ = c. 112)

Elegy

Carl Reinecke
from Op. 183

Andante con moto (♩ = c. 92)

Prelude

Carl Reinecke
from Op. 183

Moderato (♩ = c. 84)

Song

Carl Reinecke
from Op. 183

Andante con moto (♩ = c. 112)

Larghetto

Domenico Scarlatti
K. 34

ⓐ Phrase marks and dynamics are editorial.

ⓑ 

13
mf
17
mf
mp
mf
21
mf
mf
25
mf
p
f

Sonata in D Minor

Domenico Scarlatti
K. 32

Moderato cantabile (♩. = c. 48)

ⓐ Dynamics are editorial.

Andante

Franz Schubert

(♩ = c. 112)

Chorale

Robert Schumann
Op. 68, No. 4

A Famous Melody by Beethoven

(Alternate title: Joyful, Joyful We Adore Thee)

Con forza, festosamente (♩ = c. 138)

Robert Schumann

Little Cradle Song

(Alternate title: Song)

Robert Schumann
Op. 124, No. 6

Not fast (♩ = c. 100)

25
29
rit.
dim.
in Tempo
33
37
41
45
dim.

Little Study

(Alternate title: Meditation)

Robert Schumann
Op. 124, No. 6

Gently and very even (♩ = c. 100)

ⓐ Schumann's original pedal markings.

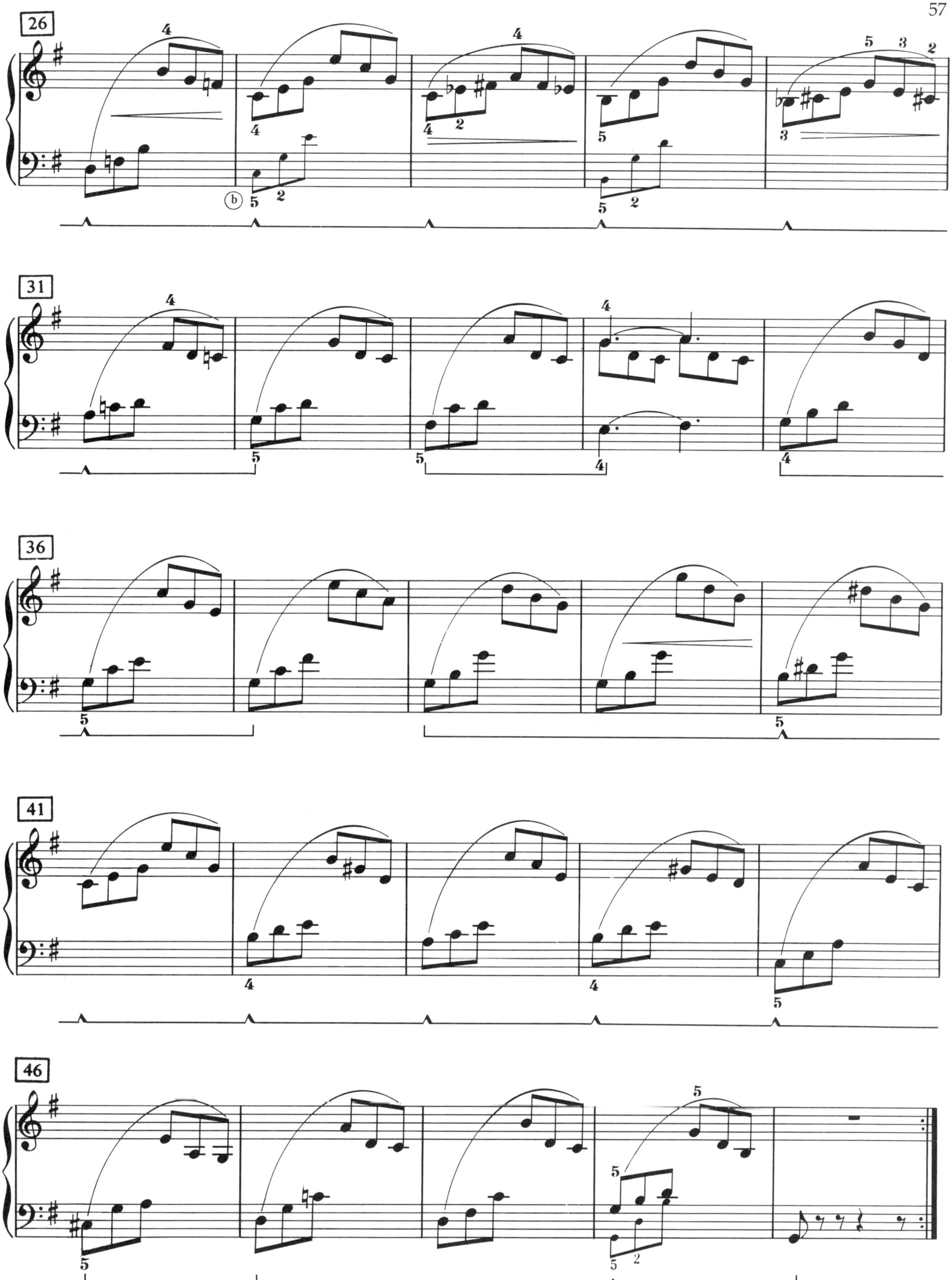

ⓑ The small notes in measures 27, 29 and 49 are optional.

Melody

Robert Schumann
Op. 68, No. 1

(a) Fingerings in italics are Schumann's

Norse Song

(Alternate title: Prelude to Worship)

Robert Schumann
Op. 68, No. 40

In folk style (♩ = c. 76)

In Church

Peter Ilyich Tchaikowsky
Op. 39, No. 24

Moderato (♩ = c. 76)

25
p
pp
31
pp
37
43
pp
perdendosi
48
ppp

Serious Feelings

(Alternate title: Adagio)

Daniel Gottlob Türk

Adagio (♩ = c. 72)

ⓐ Dynamics are editorial.

ⓑ 

Andantino

Johann George Witthauer

ⓐ Dynamics are editorial.